D1742043

1 MONTH OF
FREE
READING

at
www.ForgottenBooks.com

By purchasing this book you are eligible for one month membership to ForgottenBooks.com, giving you unlimited access to our entire collection of over 1,000,000 titles via our web site and mobile apps.

To claim your free month visit:

www.forgottenbooks.com/free948349

ISBN 978-0-260-44087-7
PIBN 10948349

Conservationist
CONTENTS

**BY
DAVE
MORELAND**

Several factors can influence hunter success and overall deer sightings during a season. In Louisiana, weather is probably the prime factor in hunter success. In general, when the temperature is warm (above 60 degrees), deer movement is poor. Deer put on their winter coats in the fall to protect themselves from cold temperatures. This cold weather requires the deer to feed more frequently because their bodies are using up more energy to stay warm. Deer become less active when the temperature is warm, and much of their movement occurs at night when it is more comfortable to move around. A look back at the 2003-04 deer season should provide insight for hunter success in the 2004-05 season.

A review of the weather conditions across the state during the 2003-04 season follows (see chart at right):

November was the important month for hunters in Areas 2, 3, 7 and 8. The mild weather during the peak of the rut no doubt had an impact on deer sightings and hunter success. The cold weather that came in December and January came too late.

By late December, bucks are losing their antlers in these areas of the state. The cold weather in December and January should have helped the Area 1, 4, 5 and 6 hunters.

WEEK	AVERAGE STATE TEMPERATURE	REMARKS
Sept. 29-Oct. 5	60-70 degrees	Oct. 3, low 40
Oct. 6-12	70 degrees	wet week
Oct. 13-19	60-70-80 degrees	dry and pleasant week
Oct. 27-Nov. 2	65 degrees	warmer than normal
Nov. 3-9	67 degrees, 80 on some days	unusually warm
Nov. 10-16	64 degrees, low 30 on 14th	heavy rain at end of week but 80 degrees high on some days
Nov. 17-23	64 degrees	6 degrees above normal
Nov. 24-30	50 degrees	first fall freeze
Dec. 1-7	51 degrees	very cold on 5th & 6th
Dec. 8-14	48 degrees	very cold on 11th & 12th
Dec. 15-22	47 degrees	two cold fronts
Dec. 22-28	52 degrees	70 degree temp. on some days
Dec. 29- Jan. 4	58 degrees	10 degrees above normal
Jan. 5-11	44 degrees	coldest weather to date
Jan. 12-18	55 degrees	8 degrees above normal, normally the coldest week of the year
Jan. 19-25	47 degrees	last week of gun hunting
Jan. 26-Feb. 1	46 degrees	last week of bow hunting

These cold fronts that came in December and early January, however, lasted only a day or two, and this made it difficult to pattern deer. The last two weeks of January provided hunters with the most consistent cold weather and should have benefited the Area 6 hunters.

The reproductive data collected from herd health checks this spring indicate that breeding activity this past season may have been a little later than normal. Breeding dates for two does in Area 1 in southeast Louisiana were January 3 and 15. Breeding dates for three does from Pointe Coupee Parish, Area 6, were February 3, 4 and 10. The later season that is being planned for Area 6 in 2004 should help hunters in this area.

Other factors influencing hunter success and overall deer sightings include habitat changes on a tract of land, mast abundance (which impacts deer utilization at food plots and feeders), annual changes in deer populations due to reproductive success (or lack of success) and hunter disturbance during the season.

Mast production across the state this past fall was mainly limited to the red oak group (water, willow, cherrybark, Southern red and nuttall). Acorn production from the white oak group (white oak, cow oak, overcup oak and post oak) was low, although some white oak mast was available in a few localized areas around the state. Examination of deer stomachs revealed high utilization of red oak acorns around the state. No doubt hunters who concentrated their efforts primarily on food plots and feeders probably did not experience high success, especially when the acorns were falling. The mild October and November weather also kept the native plant forage green and available for food.

The abundant rainfall in the spring and early summer of 2004 should keep the nutritional value of the native forages high. French mulberry provides both fruit and browse for deer.

Photos by Dave Moreland

How important is the mast crop to our Louisiana deer herds? A bumper crop of acorns will provide forage for deer well into spring and even summer. Stomach analyses of two deer killed by lightning in East Feliciana Parish in June 2004 found heavy use of water oak acorns. These two deer were in excellent condition and had good kidney fat levels. In July 2002, a herd health collection on Sherburne WMA found deer still eating large quantities of striped oak acorns along with muscadines and palmetto fruit.

The mast crop currently developing on the white oak and red oak groups for the fall of 2004 appears to be promising. In fact, the red oak mast crop for 2005 appears to be good also. White oak acorns develop in one growing season and the red oaks develop in two seasons.

Browse surveys conducted by department biologists this spring have found good growth and availability of native forage. The lack of rainfall this spring has certainly not been a problem in Louisiana and should maintain the nutritional value of these plants for deer. Soft mast fruits such as blackberries, red mulberries and pokeweed have been abundant. Good groceries in the woods equate to the healthy growth and development of deer.

There should be a substantial fawning season in 2004 across the state as a result of these excellent habitat conditions. In 2001 there was a notable decline in the lactation rates of adult does on both the WMAs and DMAP lands. This would mean a reduction in fawn production for 2001. These deer would now be in the two-year age class, and this could have reduced the sightings of adult does and young adult bucks. Nevertheless, productivity for 2004 appears to be high. Fawn breeding was documented for the first time in Area 6. All adult does examined in the herd health checks have been pregnant with twins.

Along with productivity, the growth and development of the antlered bucks should be better than what was found in 2003. While there were some above average bucks killed in 2003, overall antler quality was down. The upcoming season may be one of those bumper years for quality bucks. Now is the time to be getting ready for the 2004 deer season. With the excellent mast crop that appears to be developing, hunters can learn a lesson from the past seasons and focus their hunting opportunity around the oak trees rather than the food plots and feeders. 🔶

Dave Moreland is the Wildlife Division Administrator for the Louisiana Department of Wildlife and Fisheries. A regular contributor to Louisiana Conservationist, he is also an official measurer for the Boone and Crockett Club, the Pope and Young Club and the Longhunter Society.

Annual herd health checks use body fat as an indicator of animal health. This assessment is based upon the percent of kidney fat present. These two deer that were killed by lightning had good levels of kidney fat and were in excellent condition.

Photos by Dave Moreland

Below, C.R. Newland, an official Boone & Crockett measurer with LDWF, measures the length of the main beam on this nice buck. Antler quality was down in 2003 but is expected to be much better in 2004.

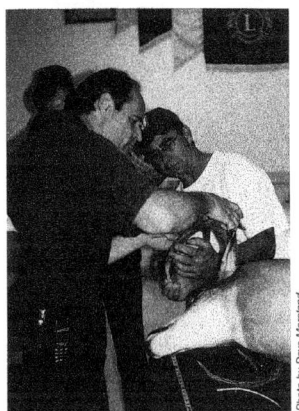

Photo by Dave Moreland

Photo by Dave Moreland

Above, Mark Dugas killed this fine buck with a bow and arrow in Concordia Parish this past season. The buck will qualify for both the state and Pope & Young record books.

Top 10 Trophy and Recognition Bucks Officially Scored
2003-2004 HUNTING SEASON

SCORE	PARISH	AREA	DATE	HUNTER	WEAPON
171	Vernon	3	10/27/03	Donald Collins	Gun
152 2/8	Union	2	11/21/03	Benny Modisette	Gun
152 2/8	Rapides	2	12/01/03	William Branch	Bow & Arrow
149 4/8	Bossier	2	12/05/03	Michael Guyton	Gun
148 6/8	Concordia	1	12/03	Johnny Vead	Muzzleloader
148 4/8	E. Feliciana	1	11/02/03	Bill Fromenthal	Bow & Arrow
146 5/8	W. Feliciana	1	10/01/03	Owen Triche	Bow & Arrow
146 3/8	Concordia	1	12/10/03	Mark Dugas	Bow & Arrow
144 1/8	Claiborne	2	11/05/03	Joe Heckel	Gun
137 7/8	Rapides	6	12/03	Tommy Klar	Gun

BY
SCOTT
DURHAM

As I topped the long rise of a hill in the battered old loaner Nebraska state truck, the still-low morning sun cast soft light across the vast sea of gray-brown plowed earth. To my right, less than a mile away, a huge splash of white formed a crescent around a shallow wetland and contrasted against the dark prairie soils that help feed the world. My pulse quickened as I looked for a place to pull over out of sight. Fortunately there was a dense woody hedgerow that ran right up to the gravel road and was part of the drain that ran to the wetland. I slid out of the truck and quietly shut the door. I slipped my hip boots on, grabbed a small backpack and crouched low to begin the approach.

Only 10 minutes later and nearly in range, I began to hear the low roar of the approaching jet. The light geese began working their wings, nervous, heads up, all facing the wind. And then they flushed, first 10 then 100, then another 500 and then in rapid successional waves, all 30,000 Snow Geese, only yards away coming right back over my head in a white and blue-grey whirring of wings with high pitched barking calls and goose talk. They spiraled around up into the clean midwestern air and disappeared over the hill. Disappointed but amazed at the same time, I slowly put my spotting scope back into my pack, stood up straight and went back to the pickup.

It's always good to be in new country. But the opportunity to do wildlife work in new habitats is even better. In early March 2004, Louisiana Department of Wildlife and Fisheries biologists assisted the Canadian Wildlife Service and the Nebraska Game and Parks Commission with goose collar observations many miles from home. Neck collars on geese, like leg bands, provide survival rates, migration routes and other important information for biologists charged with managing the continent's migratory waterfowl.

However, with goose collar observations, the bird does not have to be harvested or actually recaptured to gain the information. The code on a neck collar is a combination of numbers and letters and can be read with a good spotting scope from a quarter mile away; amazingly, the same goose can be seen in Canada, Nebraska, Louisiana and points in between during the same winter. Neck collar observations and band returns have revealed that many geese that winter in Louisiana and that use the Mississippi Flyway for their winter migration use the eastern edge of the Central Flyway for their return trip to the breeding grounds.

The Rainwater Basin of southcentral and southeast Nebraska lies in the Central Flyway and is a famous spring migration stopover area for millions of waterfowl, shorebirds and Sandhill Cranes. In addition to vast numbers of Light Geese, it is estimated that 30 percent of the continental Pintail population, 50 percent of the mid-continent Mallard population and 90 percent of the mid-continent White-front population use the basin before continuing to their nesting grounds. Some Mallards, Blue-winged Teal and other species remain in the area to nest and rear young. Hundreds of thousands of cranes, Snow, White-fronted and Canada geese feed in harvested cornfields where grain is left after combining. The geese use precious wetlands within the vast agricultural landscape for loafing and roosting. At one time, these wetlands were very numerous, hence the name of the region.

Today, as in other areas of North America, agricultural producers trying to maximize production on their lands usually farm as much acreage as possible. Therefore, many of these wetlands have fallen to the plow. Center-pivot irrigation has dramatically multiplied corn yields but further caused the loss of grasslands to farming and dramatically lowered the water table. The famous Platte River now normally flows at only 25 percent of its original volume. Economics and consumer demand for marbled beef and other corn-based products make irrigated corn farming even in semiarid regions more profitable than maintaining native prairie grassland for free range beef production, although a few niche markets have recently appeared. In northwest Nebraska, in a region not suitable to tillage farming, a large portion of native prairie still exists. Buffalo are once more grazing much of it.

Little on the North American continent affects waterfowl and other wildlife populations like federal (Farm Bill) and provincial farm policies and agricultural practices. In the Rainwater Basin, only 374 of the historical 4,000 wetland basins remain and the acreage has been reduced from 100,000 to 22,000. The buildup of silt, changes in water distribution and invasive plants have also affected remaining wetland quality. But although historically fewer, impressive numbers of waterfowl still come. Some of the remaining wetlands constitute, or are within, federal waterfowl production areas or state wildlife management areas. These lands are managed for waterfowl and other wildlife through techniques such as prescribed burning, moist soil manipulations, grazing and haying.

Disease outbreaks such as avian cholera are more likely to occur when large numbers of waterfowl crowd into relatively small areas, a situation that remains a concern for managers. To help reduce disease risk and to meet the energetic and habitat needs of migratory and nesting waterbirds using the Rainwater Basin, science-based wetland acquisitions through the North American Wetlands Conservation Act and the Rainwater Basin Joint Venture are critical.

To read goose collars, we cruised the long gravel roads laid out in section-line fashion in search of large flocks of geese. This year would be one in which many of the geese would not stop over for very long due to dry conditions or other variables; and numbers were down. Even so, groups of up to 50,000 Snows were not too hard to find. We mostly worked out of pickups, and tried to position the sun and wind to our backs. We hoped for overcast days to reduce the visual distortion caused by shimmering heat waves reflected off of the plowed earth.

Neck collars, like the ones on these Snow geese, provide survival rates, migration routes and other important information.

Photo courtesy of Jon Einar Jónsson

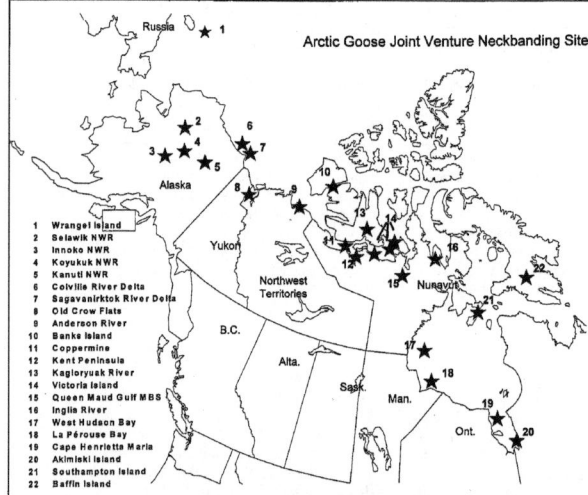

Arctic Goose Joint Venture Neckbanding Sites

Russia

Alaska

Yukon

Northwest
Territories

B.C.

Alta.

Sask.

Man.

Ont.

Nunavut

1   Wrangel Island
2   Selawik NWR
3   Innoko NWR
4   Koyukuk NWR
5   Kanuti NWR
6   Colville River Delta
7   Sagavanirktok River Delta
8   Old Crow Flats
9   Anderson River
10 Banks Island
11 Coppermine
12 Kent Peninsula
13 Kagloryuak River
14 Victoria Island
15 Queen Maud Gulf MBS
16 Inglis River
17 West Hudson Bay
18 La Pérouse Bay
19 Cape Henrietta Maria
20 Akimiski Island
21 Southampton Island
22 Baffin Island

affecting other species here in the basin and on their Arctic breeding grounds was in progress, and Snow Geese were being hunted a few days a week. On a couple of these days, it was extremely difficult to get in range, even with our spotting scopes. On days when the wind was gusting to 25 knots or more, it was difficult to keep the scope still enough to read collars.

Since 1987, 129,776 Lesser Snow, Ross', White-fronted and small Canada geese have been neck-collared in North America. The vast majority of these collarings were done on the breeding grounds of the Canadian Arctic and Alaska. During the same time period, 30,102 goose collar observations (an average of 1,771 observations each year) have been made in Nebraska, the great majority in the basin. In comparison, 9,514 collar observations have been made in Louisiana during the wintering period.

Occasionally we were able to observe geese on ponds or lakes in large numbers. They would slowly swim around in a circular motion, and the reading was excellent. The Conservation Order season, which is an attempt to continentally reduce the numbers of Snow Geese negatively

Flock of geese in flight at Nebraska collar readings in March 2004.

Photo by Scott Durham

Photos by Scott Durham

Modern goose collars have a combination of three letters or numbers. One of the characters is vertical and two of the characters are stacked horizontally. The vertical character is read first, then the bottom horizontal character and lastly the top horizontal character. Order is therefore very important when reading the collar.

Collar reading requires skill and patience and the trip to Nebraska gave me a better appreciation of what it takes to do this kind of work well. Seeing such large flocks of geese and being able to get close enough to read collars is pure excitement. When that first hint of color catches your eye, the characters begin to come into focus. You get the number, recheck it and a sound sense of satisfaction is realized. Occasionally, three or four geese with collars on them were all in view at once. It was a challenge to get them all. Reading a rare black collar that was put on in southwest Louisiana by LSU doctoral student and waterfowl researcher Jón Jónsson was a trophy read. Reading two yellow collars put on Ross' Geese on the west coast of Hudson Bay in the Arctic by the great hunter and Olympic skeet shooter Jason Caswell of Canada was especially satisfying. Working with the department, other wildlifers and our fabulous migratory bird resources, I received high dividends. ❧

Scott Durham is the North American Waterfowl Plan Coordinator for the Louisiana Department of Wildlife and Fisheries. In his 10 years with the department, Scott has worked with habitat management, waterfowl and upland wildlife.

Nebraska corn stubble and waste corn.

LOUISIANA'S

STEEL-LEGGED REEFS

**STORY BY
JERRY
LABELLA**

**PHOTOS BY
CAPT. SCOTT
AVANZINO**

Off the coast of Louisiana lie some of the world's most productive and unusual reefs. Not the coral or shell types that most people think about when "reefs" are mentioned, but the steel-legged kind that oil production companies plant throughout the waters of the Gulf of Mexico. No doubt the early engineers of these structures gave little thought at the time of their development as to the positive impact such installations would have on marine life and the fishing community.

"Whether it's an operating oil and gas production platform or a retired platform intentionally placed for conservation and fisheries enhancement, a typical four-pile platform jacket (the underwater support structure of an offshore platform) provides two to three acres of living and feeding habitat for thousands of underwater species," according to the U.S. Department of the Interior, Mineral Management Service (MMS).

It is no wonder that many anglers are finding that these steel offshore oil production platforms draw fish like magnets. Besides harboring numerous juvenile and adult resident species, these steel-legged reefs serve as hunting grounds for swift, open-ocean pelagic fish like mackerel, tuna and jacks.

Marine researchers have reported fish densities 20 to 50 times higher at oil and gas platforms than in nearby open water, and each platform seasonally serves as critical habitat for 10,000 to 20,000 fishes, many of which are of recreational and commercial importance.

One man that knows well the fish-attracting power of offshore platforms is Captain Scott Avanzino of Paradise Charters out of Venice. He's honed the technique of catching tuna at night down to a science.

While oil-production platforms attract fish 24 hours a day, the odds of catching them increase by night due to the lighting on many of the rigs. For example, bright vapor lights often beam down to the water's surface on these structures, overshooting bridge walks, loading docks and other areas requiring illumination. "The lights of the rigs simply attract bait," Avanzino said, "and the structure which doubles as a full-time fish attracting device, coupled with the lights, serves as a nighttime beacon marking a presumed safe haven for bait fish for miles."

Avanzino particularly likes fishing deepwater platforms that are generally found throughout the blue water zone of the Gulf of Mexico. He's found that tuna have adapted to feeding under the lights not just to satisfy their constant urge to eat but because it is easy pickings.

The oil-production platforms provide an excellent setting for tuna to ambush bait fish. Here they use the cover of darkness to lie in wait for unsuspecting bait to come into their forage areas. For the yellowfin tuna, this forage area lies on the outer reaches of the upcurrent side of the platform near the surface (0 to 50 feet) where the rig light fades into natural darkness (100 to 400 yards). On the other hand, blackfin tuna prefer depths closest to the rig (50 to 100 yards) where the last reaches of penetrable surface light fade into complete darkness (100 to 200 feet).

Tuna can be found at just about any lighted rig in 300 or more feet of water. This is particularly true of blackfin tuna, while yellowfin tuna prefer deeper blue water where temperatures range between 68 and 84 degrees. These are ideal areas that draw flying fish, the preferred diet of yellowfin tuna.

Blackfin and yellowfin tuna also prefer to feed on different baits. Blackfin favor squid and yellowfin favor flying fish. To be successful, you have to employ baits and methods that imitate the specific bait for each species. Heavy chrome jigs, like the diamond jigs, imitate squid, while surface baits, like top-water poppers, imitate injured flying fish.

Blackfins are more interested in chasing squid at depths the light becomes less of a factor. Bearing this out is the fact that Avanzino has caught blackfin as far as a mile away from a rig where there was no penetrable surface light at all. The only evidence that they were there came via the fish finder display.

Avanzino believes that fishing the upcurrent side of a rig is far better than the downcurrent side. His reasoning is that there is always more surface activity and a fresh supply of flying fish and flotsam. One effective method that he uses is drifting with the grass patches toward the rig, looking for the flying fish to get flushed out of hiding. When this occurs, he casts his bait right in front of them.

Blackfins are usually easy to catch at night, so easy at times anglers can virtually sink the boat with them. They will hit anything that is moving fast on the drop or rise.

For the sheer fun and challenge, most anglers choose to use light tackle. The four-to-six ounce diamond jig in chrome or glow color is the weapon of choice. Avanzino uses 30-pound line or lighter with a medium rod in an attempt to match the tackle.

Blackfin are most often found 50 to 200 feet down and close to the rig structure where they enjoy feeding on squid. At night they come to the surface. That's why diamond jigs work so effectively; they mimic tiny squid.

Though many tuna anglers think you
have to jig the lure up and down briskly for
a strike, this really is not necessary. It just
has to be moving fast in one direction or the
other—up or down. It is as simple as drop-
ping the lure 200 feet down and then reeling it in quickly.

Comparably speaking, yellowfin tuna
are harder to catch than blackfin. To be successful, it is important to catch some live
bait. Hardtail jacks are a good choice but
they can be difficult to catch at night. The
best choice, according to Avanzino, is flying fish, either dead or live.

Most of the time a spreader light and
cast net are all that's needed, but a fisherman's green light will work wonders if you
can find a safe way to hang it off the tran-
som. Once the flying fish swim up to the
light, all you need to do is throw a cast net
to catch them.

In any case, if there's a problem with
catching flying fish, the next best alterna-
tive is to use top-water poppers. Once
again, the action is more important than
color choice. This lure is basically designed
to spit water from its cupped head as it
moves forward. Thus the trick is to get the
lure to dart through the water sporadically
with a sweeping action.

"I have seen tuna follow the bait all the
way to the boat and hit it at the very last
second," Avanzino said. "If the yellowfins
are not actively feeding, try making blind
casts at or near patches of scattered grass.
Odds are that the tuna are not too far
below."

Sometimes yellowfin can be observed
boiling the water's surface in a feeding

frenzy. When this sit-
uation is encoun-
tered, cast the bait
anywhere near them
and a successful
hookup is imminent.
If they happen to be
out of casting range,
then be sure to move
stealthily. Never
make a bold run into
or near feeding fish as
this will cause them
to disperse and go
deep.

Gear selection is
most critical when
going after these tor-
pedolike speedsters.
Avanzino uses Alutecno Albacore 50/80
reels with 650 yards of 80-pound monofila-
ment for yellowfins because the drags are
smooth, precise and dependable. It is
impossible to put the drag in free spool or
full strike without pressing a button on the
side of the reel, so there are no birdnests on
the take or during the fight and no spastic

two-thumb break-offs due to accidental over-drag once the drag has been set.

Proper drag setting is as equally essential as the right equipment. The reels are set with 27 pounds of fight drag, leaving the strike drag at about two to three pounds on the take. When a tuna grabs the bait, it is crucial to let him run for a second or two and slide the lever up to full position while reeling. When properly executed, it plants the 12/0 circle hook in the side of the mouth every time. When fishing live bait, Avanzino hooks the bait in the mouth from the bottom lip through the nostril with a Mustad 8/0 live bait hook attached to 20 feet of 130-pound fluorocarbon leader attached with a dacron loop to a bimini twist on the main line.

Though details to the specifics may vary among anglers, one thing's for sure—the fish will be there waiting at Louisiana's steel-legged reefs.

Jerry LaBella is a writer, photographer and avid fisherman from Kenner, Louisiana. You can visit him on the web at www.jerrylabella.com.

THE LOUISIANA ARTIFICIAL REEF PROGRAM

The Louisiana Artificial Reef Program was established in 1986 to take advantage of obsolete oil and gas platforms which were recognized as an important habitat to many of Louisiana's coastal fishes. Federal law and international treaty require these platforms to be removed one year after production ceases, at great expense to the industry. The removal of these platforms results in a loss of reef habitat.

Since the program's inception in 1986, 24 different petroleum companies have participated in the program, donating the jackets of 85 structures. In addition to the material, the participating companies also contributed over $12.2 million into Louisiana's Artificial Reef Trust Fund, which also represents a similar saving on platform abandonment to the industry. In 1998, six projects across the coast were completed. Recently the Louisiana program created the world's largest artificial reef from the Freeport sulfur mine off Grand Isle, Louisiana. The sulfur mine, with over 1.5 miles of bridgework, is composed of more than 29 structures ranging from four-pile bridge supports to a 35-pile power plant. The reef is in 60 feet of water and has 30 feet of clearance. For safety of navigation it is marked by five lighted buoys. The reef program also developed reefs in Louisiana's inshore waters, primarily low profile reefs composed of shell.

For photos, maps and locations, visit the LDWF website at *www.wlf.louisiana.gov* or contact Rick Kasprzak, Program Supervisor at 225/765-2375.

Photo by Thomas Gresham

Project
Clean-Up

Inmate Crew Collects Litter On Alexander State Forest WMA

On a sunny July morning, a group of men arrive at Alexander State Forest Wildlife Management Area, managed by the Louisiana Department of Wildlife and Fisheries, near Alexandria. They are not there to fish the adjacent Indian Creek Reservoir or hike through the pine forest. The men are part of "Project Clean-Up," a statewide litter collection program.

"Project Clean-Up," administered by the Department of Public Safety and Corrections and the Department of Transportation and Development in cooperation with the Office of the Governor, involves inmate crews from all state adult institutions and local crews from seven parishes. They work an average of 15,000 man-hours per week, mostly collecting litter from highways.

The men at Alexander State Forest WMA are inmates of the J. Levy Dabadie Correctional Center (DCC), a minimum-security facility on the grounds of the Louisiana National Guard Camp Beauregard. "From time to time, usually before and after hunting season, someone from (the Louisiana Department of Wildlife and Fisheries) will contact us to send a crew to collect trash and debris," said DCC Warden T.W. Thompson. Region Biologist Bill Burns, who supervises the upkeep of the area WMAs, contacts the warden when cleanup is necessary.

"We are indebted to DCC," said LDWF Secretary Dwight Landreneau. "The work that their crews perform helps keep our natural areas pristine."

The partnership between DCC and LDWF has been ongoing for more than 15 years. The inmate crews help with the upkeep of six LDWF sites in central Louisiana. Warden Thompson said, "We are always happy to partner with state agencies on public service projects."

"Project Clean-Up" was started in 1996 under the Foster administration and continues under Governor Blanco. From January 2004 through the week of July 8, 2004, the 12 adult state institutions have covered 12,416 miles of roadway, collecting 163,412 bags of trash and expending 142,259 inmate manhours.

Inmate crews from all state adult institutions pick up bag refuse along roadways while being supervised by correctional officers. Then, DOTD work crews pick up the bags and mow. The Department of Corrections also helps with clean-up efforts for special events. Crews clean out ditches, mow grass and perform general maintenance tasks in public areas and for non-profit agencies across the state. Public service work performed for the same period described above are 271,228 inmate manhours with 26,936 bags of trash collected and a . distance of 2,848 miles covered. The miles covered in these areas are fewer because crews are usually working in one concentrated area, such as the wildlife management areas like the one at Alexander State Forest. ✦

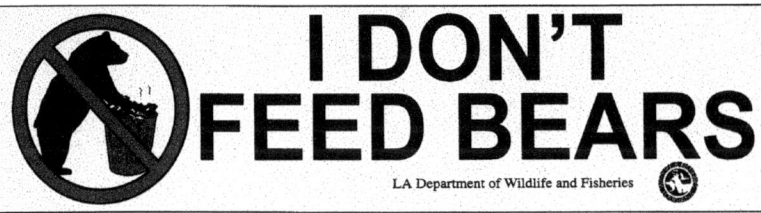

LA Department of Wildlife and Fisheries

New Law Prohibits Feeding of Bears

One act of this past legislative session was to pass a bill that will outlaw the feeding of wild bears. Maria Davidson, a senior field biologist for the Louisiana Department of Wildlife and Fisheries, helped draft the bill and is optimistic that it will help the department's efforts to restore Louisiana's bear population.

"Prohibiting bear feeding will allow us to fulfill our mission of managing this wildlife resource responsibly by protecting bears as well as the public," said Davidson.

Act No. 164 reads, "No person shall intentionally feed or attempt to feed a wild bear. The provisions of this Section shall not prohibit legal baiting of deer. The first violation of this Section by any person shall result in the issuance of a warning ticket only. Any subsequent violation by the same person shall be a class two violation. The Wildlife and Fisheries Commission is authorized to promulgate, under the Administrative Procedure Act, rules and regulations for the administration and enforcement of this Section."

Louisiana black bears are normally secretive and shy around people, but they will lose their fear of humans once they begin to associate them with food. The majority of bear complaints that LDWF receives stem from purposeful or incidental bear feeding. While no complaints have been made regarding bears being aggressive toward humans, the bear population is increasing and people are moving into areas inhabited by the bears.

"It is imperative that we be proactive to avoid conditioning bears to human foods and the negative repercussions that follow," said Davidson.

With the passage of Act 164, Louisiana joins the 12 other states where feeding bears is outlawed. Among them are Alaska, Arkansas, Colorado, Florida, Montana, New Jersey, New York, Pennsylvania, South Carolina, Vermont, Virginia and West Virginia. An additional 26 states promote educational "Do Not Feed Bears" programs.

For more information, contact Maria Davidson at 225/765-2385 (mdavidson@wlf.louisiana.gov).

While the new law targets intentional feeding of bears, avoiding bear problems also means being mindful of accidental feedings. Bears will return to any place they find something to eat. You can prevent or correct bear problems by following these guidelines:

- Never leave your garbage outside overnight. (Double bag garbage and keep it indoors.)
- Do not put garbage carts out on the street the night before pickup. Put them out the day of collection.
- Clean out your garbage cart and rinse with bleach or ammonia to cut down on food odors.
- Do not leave pet food out overnight. Feed your pets and then pick up any food that is not eaten.
- Do not leave any bait outside overnight.
- Remove all bird feeders.

If you see a bear in your yard, DO NOT FEED IT OR APPROACH IT. DO MAKE LOUD NOISES (beat on pots and pans, blow an air horn, scream and clap your hands) to attempt to scare it away.

Celebrate the gre
Louisiana Department

Saturday, September 25, 2004
9 a.m. until 3 p.m.

FREE admission!! FREE samples
of Louisiana game and seafood dishes!!

Spend a day in the great
outdoors and try something new!

Bring your family, bring your friends!

PRESENTED BY The Louisiana
Department of Wildlife and Fisheries

SPONSORED BY Coca-Cola, The Advocate,
Associated Grocers, Progressive Insurance and
Louisiana Wildlife Agents Association

utdoors with the
Wildlife and Fisheries!

ACTIVITIES: Canoeing, Fishing Clinic, Sports Shooting (Instructors present), Archery Target Shooting, Duck & Goose Calling Contest, Boating Education

DEMONSTRATIONS: Bowhunting, Fly Casting, Fly Tying, Falconry

EXHIBITS: Ducks Unlimited, LA Wildlife Federation, Operation Game Thief, Louisiana Artificial Reef Program, Audubon Society, Coastal Conservation Association, Louisiana Department of Environmental Quality, Louisiana Department of Natural Resources, Louisiana Natural Freshwater Catfish Association, Bayou State Bowhunters Association

This Year Baton Rouge Celebrates 20 Years of National Hunting & Fishing Day Events!

Activities and exhibits vary by location. Call the LDWF office in your area for more details on events throughout the state:

Baton Rouge 225/765-2925

Monroe 318/343-4044

Minden 318/371-3050

Woodworth 318/484-2212

State Wildlife Grants

**BY
STEPHEN
SORENSEN**

By the early 20th century, many of America's once numerous game species were on the verge of becoming forever lost. Factors contributing to these declines included market and unregulated hunting as well as habitat destruction. In the 1930s, this situation started to change. Wildlife and fish populations began to rebound as harvests were better regulated, wildlife management areas and refuges were created, and game species populations were augmented or restored with transplanted animals. Much of these efforts were funded by sportsmen through hunting and fishing licenses and by excise taxes placed on hunting and fishing equipment under the Pittman-Robertson (P/R) Act (Wildlife Restoration Program) and later the Wallop-Breaux/Dingle-Johnson (W/B-D/J) Acts (Sport Fish Restoration Program).

But despite these successes, very little attention was given to wildlife species which were not hunted or fished. As time

wore on, numerous non-game species were recognized as being in serious decline and some were on the verge of becoming extinct. In 1966 Congress passed the Endangered Species Preservation Act. The act was the first to provide for listing of native fish and wildlife species as threatened or endangered; it also authorized limited habitat acquisition. In 1969 the Endangered Species Conservation Act was ratified. It expanded the list of threatened and endangered species to include invertebrates and international species. The act also prohibited the import of listed species. In 1973 the Endangered Species Act (ESA) was endorsed by bipartisan majorities in Congress and signed into law by President Richard Nixon on December 28, 1973. Upon signing the ESA, President Nixon stated, "Nothing is more priceless and more worthy of preservation than the rich array of animal life with which our country has been blessed." With the creation of these laws, steps were being taken to reverse the decline of non-game species. Today, species such as the black-footed ferret, American alligator, Peregrine Falcon, grey wolf and the Bald Eagle are all on their way to once again being healthy and viable components of our natural landscape.

While the creation of the ESA was a move in the right direction for the restoration of imperiled fish and wildlife species, it still followed a path of reactive management and has proven to be very costly. For a species to receive attention, it had to be in serious decline or possibly on the brink of extinction. Something needed to be done to stem the decline of wildlife species before they reached that critical point. This required a proactive approach to wildlife management. The state game and fish agencies were recognized as the logical choice for implementing such an endeavor because of their statutory or constitutional authority to protect and manage both game and non-game wildlife. Not only does a proactive approach make better sense, it also allows for scarce conservation dollars to be used more efficiently in the restoration of all wildlife species.

Two New Programs

Over the last four years, Congress has appropriated roughly $325 million towards two new federal funding programs that are specifically designed to take a proactive approach to fish and wildlife species management and to address the continuing decline of wildlife species in all 50 states, the District of Columbia and the five territories of Puerto Rico, Guam, the Virgin Islands, American Samoa and the Northern Mariana Islands. This funding was a direct result of "Teaming With Wildlife" efforts sustained for more than a decade by fish and wildlife conservation interests across the country. Both programs were created as a compromise to the defeat of the Conservation and Reinvestment Act of 2000 (H.R. 701), otherwise known as CARA.

The first program was titled the Wildlife Conservation and Restoration Program (WCRP) and was created as a sub-account under the Pittman-Robertson Act. Congress appropriated $50 million for WCRP within the Commerce, Justice, State Appropriation Act for fiscal year 2001. As stipulated in the legislation, WCRP funds were to be used for "priority funding for those species with the greatest conservation need as defined by the State or Territory's (game and fish) program." Funds were also allowed for "wildlife associated recreation" and "wildlife conservation education," activities not found in the existing Wildlife Restoration (Pittman-Robertson Act) portion of the Federal Aid program. Funding for this program was distributed under a formula-based apportionment to states and territories similar to that in the existing Sport Fish and Wildlife Restoration Programs.

The second program was titled the State Wildlife Grants Program (SWG). Congress appropriated $50 million for SWG within the Interior Appropriation Act for fiscal year 2001. Language in the act stipulated that SWG funding "will provide funds to states for on-the-ground conservation projects that implement existing or future planning efforts to stabilize, restore, enhance and protect species and habitats of conservation concern." Funding for the first year of this program was to be competitively awarded. In the second year of the funding program, it was changed to the same formula-based apportionment as WCRP funds.

Unlike the Wildlife Restoration Program and Sport Fish Restoration Program, which have continuous funding, SWG must be reappropriated every year and funding is not guaranteed at the same level year after year. WCRP was a one-time program and has not been reauthorized by congress.

WCRP and SWG in Louisiana

As of January 1, 2004, the Louisiana Department of Wildlife and Fisheries has received $3.7 million to fund conservation activities within the state for a wide array of wildlife species and their habitats through the WCRP and SWG programs.

LDWF has made a commitment to use these funds for the conservation of those "species of greatest conservation concern" in Louisiana. The primary source of information regarding which species are most in need of conservation action comes from data in the database of our Louisiana Natural Heritage Program (LNHP).

To date there are 20 active projects underway covering several animal taxa groups, all areas of the state and ranging in scale from ecosystems to small-scale habitats that are critical for the survival of wildlife species. The projects vary in length from one to three years and include assessing the forestry management practices on 20 of our state wildlife management areas and the effect these practices have on songbirds, amphibians and reptiles; state-wide research on current bat populations (with the verification of a recent discovery of a species new to Louisiana); identifying breeding and roosting sites for Swallow-tailed Kites; state-wide surveys of small streams and bayous for fish, crawfish and mussel species; identifying critical breeding locations and migration patterns for gulf sturgeon; a survey to inventory the fish assemblages within eight of the major river systems of Louisiana; partnering with the Aquarium of the Americas to rescue and rehabilitate stranded marine mammals and sea turtles; working with timber companies and other large landowners to implement a safe harbor program for the endangered Red-cockaded Woodpecker and developing methods to manage for the endangered Louisiana pine snake; studying the breeding and wintering habitat for grassland sparrows in the Florida parishes; updating the Natural Heritage's endangered species database; and intra-agency workshops which provide department biologists a chance to update their knowledge of non-game species issues.

The Department of Wildlife and Fisheries recognized from the start that with the limited funding and manpower

resources available to the department we were not able to undertake many of the projects we felt were important to the conservation of wildlife and fish species. As a result, most of these projects have been contracted to several in-state and some out-of-state universities which have been able to provide the matching funds needed to make these studies possible. An added benefit is that it allows for current graduate student biologists to receive training they will need to address the continuing issues of biodiversity and species conservation which they will face in their future.

The Comprehensive Wildlife Conservation Strategy

In the creation of these grant programs, congress specified that every state that receives this funding be committed to the creation and development of a state-wide comprehensive wildlife conservation strategy and submit this strategy to the U.S. Fish and Wildlife Agency for approval by October 1, 2005.

Congress further stipulated that four statutory elements must be satisfied in order for a state or territory to be ranked as eligible to receive these funds:

1) The state fish and wildlife agency must have the authority to develop and implement the CWCS. Such authority should cover both game and non-game species as well as authority to undertake wildlife-associated recreation and wildlife-conservation education projects.

2) Eligible projects include the development and implementation of new wildlife conservation projects and/or projects that supplement existing wildlife programs, with appropriate consideration to all wildlife and a priority for those species with the greatest conservation need.

3) The state must show how it involved the public in the development, revision and implementation of the program or strategy and how it intends to involve the public in the development of the CWCS.

4) In the development of the CWCS, the following eight required elements are to be addressed:

• Information on the distribution and abundance of species of wildlife, including low and declining populations as the state fish and wildlife agency deems appropriate, that are indicative of the diversity and health of the state's wildlife.

Funded by SWG, LDWF's Safe Harbor Program works with landowners to manage habitat for the endangered Red-cockaded Woodpecker.

Photo by Emlyn Smith

• Descriptions of locations and relative condition of key habitats and community types essential to conservation of species.
• Descriptions of problems which may adversely affect species or their habitats, and priority research and survey efforts needed to identify factors which may assist in restoration and improved conservation of these species and habitats.
• Descriptions of conservation actions determined to be necessary to conserve the identified species and habitats and priorities for implementing such actions.
• Proposed plans for monitoring species and their habitats, for monitoring the effectiveness of the conservation actions proposed and for adapting these conservation actions to respond appropriately to new information or changing conditions.
• Descriptions of procedures to review the strategy at intervals not to exceed ten years.
• Plans for coordinating, to the extent feasible, the development, implementation, review and revision of the strategy with federal, state and local agencies and Indian tribes that manage significant land and water areas within the state or administer programs that significantly affect the conservation of identified species and habitats.
• Provisions for broad public participation in the development and implementation of the strategy.

We have begun the process for developing this strategy and hope to have it completed by July 2005. A core committee of LDWF personnel has been organized and representatives from every division are participating. Early drafts of the strategy will be sent out to other federal and state agencies, academia and non-governmental organizations to gather their input. We aim to develop a plan that reflects the needs of species at risk in Louisiana and the desires of key constituent groups, partners and staff in protecting and enhancing our valuable wildlife resources.

The State Wildlife Grants program provides the funding states need to prevent wildlife species from becoming endangered. The fundamental goal of the program is to keep common species common. Through early, strategic intervention, we can recover declining wildlife populations and prevent future conflicts over endangered species listings.

We hope that everyone with an interest in Louisiana's fish and wildlife resources will be pleased with our decisions.

LDWF File Photo

Although we may not address every important need in the first draft, we look at this as the beginning of a new direction in the management of all species of fish and wildlife in Louisiana. ⌇

Stephen Sorensen is a graduate of LSU with a degree in wildlife management. Having worked with neotropical migrant songbirds, Louisiana black bears and songbird breeding studies, he is currently the State Wildlife Grant Coordinator for LDWF.

SWG monies also support research on the rare and secretive Louisiana pine snake.

**BY MAJOR
JEFF MAYNE**

When the legislature comes to Baton Rouge, not many people think of issues related to wildlife and fisheries. During the 2004 regular session of the Louisiana Legislature, the department tracked and monitored over 200 legislative instruments throughout the legislative process. In addition to bills filed by legislators on behalf of constituents or themselves, the department also puts together its own legislative package approved by the Governor's Office to take care of statutory problems which arise, eliminate loopholes, make things simpler for the people who participate in activities regulated by our department and better manage, protect and conserve our state's valuable natural resources.

The Department of Wildlife and Fisheries recognizes the complexities of the laws which regulate our state's natural resources. We strive to simplify them while maximizing public participation and the economic benefit derived from the legal utilization while balancing the overall protection of the resource.

In addition to other acts which were passed during the session, the voting public will have an opportunity to make the final decision on an amendment to the state's constitution preserving the freedom to hunt, fish and trap wildlife including all aquatic life, traditionally taken by hunters, trappers and anglers. The amendment further emphasized that such freedom is a valued natural heritage that shall be forever preserved for the people of Louisiana. This proposition to amend the constitution will be on the ballot for the elections held on November 2, 2004.

While many people are not affected in any way by these legislative changes, what follows is a brief synopsis of some of the bills, which were passed into acts during the 2004 Regular Session of the Louisiana Legislature.

Licenses

Act 835 creates a lifetime senior hunting and fishing license for a fee of $50 for persons over the age of 60 who are required to otherwise purchase the annual $5 senior hunting and fishing license. This new lifetime license eliminates annual license purchases and includes basic hunting, big game, bow and muzzleloader, state waterfowl and turkey hunting stamps and the basic and saltwater fishing license privileges. This act also establishes a "saltwater fisheries enforcement account" in which contributions, donations or court awards may be made dedicated specifically to aid in the enforcement efforts related to saltwater fisheries enforcement activities.

Act 237 changes the recreational possession limit for catfish caught in Toledo Bend Reservoir from 100 to 125 per day and allows 50 of the 125 to be taken and possessed under the minimum recreational size limit.

Fishing

Act 240 removes the requirement of crab trap floats on crab traps used in the freshwater areas of the state which are north of the northern bank of the Intracoastal Waterway and west of LA Highway 70.

Act 831 establishes a moratorium on the purchase of commercial crab trap gear licenses. Commercial crab trap gear licenses for license year 2005 can only be purchased by commercial crabbers who held commercial crab trap gear licenses for one of the years 2002, 2003 or 2004.

Act 86 allows the use of commercial shad seines to be used at night in St. Landry Parish, the Whiskey Bay Pilot Channel and portions of the Atchafalaya and Mississippi River from February 1 through June 30 of each year. The act also allows commercial fishermen using shad seines to take of other types of legal size commercial fish.

Act 825 allows shad and skipjack to be taken with a special commercial gill net in Lake Palourde and Lake Verret. The act also moves the existing boundary line for the recreational use of hoop nets and wire nets from US 190 to I-10 in the eastern portion of the state. This line move allows more area for recreational fisherman to utilize these types of gear.

Act 211 provides that persons convicted of certain oyster harvesting violations be required to have vessel monitoring systems attached to their vessels so the department can monitor their fishing activities.

Act 97 requires that commercial nets attached to a wharf or camp being used to harvest shrimp be tagged by the department identifying gear licensure and the identity of the person fishing the net.

Act 904 creates the "Shrimp Trade Petition Account" where commercial shrimp fishermen and dealers will contribute to the expenses incurred for the imposition of antidumping duties on foreign shrimp.

Hunting

Act 100 simplifies requirements relative to the supervision of persons hunting who are under 16. The act removes the requirement that persons under the age of 16 complete a hunter safety education course in order to participate in a special youth deer hunting season when under the direct supervision of either an adult who possesses a valid hunting license or a person who is at least 18.

Act 841 provides that the Wildlife and Fisheries Commission may promulgate and adopt rules and regulations to establish a deer and turkey tagging/record and reporting system. The commission may only adopt the tagging/record system for deer when a reduced buck harvest is initiated. A tagging/record system for turkey could be established for the 2006 hunting season.

Act 849 requires the Department of Wildlife and Fisheries to keep at least one all terrain vehicle trail open throughout the year on department owned wildlife management areas. This requirement is based on weather safety and environmental conditions and requires the possession of a WMA permit for trail utilization.

Boating

Act 238 establishes "no-wake" zones within 300 feet of a public boat launch or a docking facility associated with a public boat launch. "No wake" requires that each vessel operate at bare steerage speed, the slowest speed the vessel can travel to produce the minimum water surface turbulence while allowing the operator to maintain directional control of the vessel.

Act 709 adjusts the minimum age requirements of persons who are authorized to operate personal watercrafts (jet skis). The new law establishes that persons under the age of 16 may not operate a personal watercraft. However, the act grandfathers in those persons who are 13 by January 1, 2005, and who have successfully completed a boater education course, allowing them to continue to operate personal watercrafts.

Miscellaneous

Act 253 changed the adjudication process for class one wildlife and fisheries offenses (minor violations) from being administered by the Division of Administrative Law to being administered in local district courts.

Act 865 creates the Louisiana Aquaculture Coordinating Council within the Department of Agriculture and Forestry. The act transfers regulation of aquacultural activities from being exclusively regulated by the Department of Wildlife and Fisheries and the Wildlife and Fisheries Commission to being jointly regulated by the Department of Agriculture and Forestry and the Department of Wildlife and Fisheries. The Commissioner of Agriculture and the Wildlife and Fisheries Commission will promulgate rules and regulations for aquacultural activities.

Act 164 prohibits the intentional feeding of bears in the wild.

Act 174 requires that $2 from every fine imposed by courts on persons who violated wildlife and fisheries regulations to be deposited into a reward fund. The reward fund will be used as a community-oriented policing project to encourage individuals to report criminal activity regarding wildlife and fisheries violations to the department's enforcement division.

Act 613 establishes the White Lake Property Fund as a special fund in the state's treasury within the Louisiana Wildlife and Fisheries Conservation Fund. This act also establishes the White Lake Property Advisory Board within the Department of Wildlife and Fisheries and requires the board to advise the Louisiana Wildlife and Fisheries Commission and the Department of Wildlife and Fisheries on

the following matters concerning the White Lake Property provides the Louisiana Wildlife and Fisheries Commission with additional duties, responsibilities and powers to establish a conservation management plan for the White Lake Property and to authorize the conduct of lottery hunts on the White Lake Property. The act also provides the Department of Wildlife and Fisheries with additional duties, responsibilities and powers to administer, control and manage the White Lake Property.

Act 175 adds several waterways to the state natural and scenic rivers system: (1) Ouiska Chitto Creek—that portion in Beauregard Parish (2) Barnes Creek—from La. Hwy. 27 to the Calcasieu River in Allen and Beauregard parishes (3) Beckwith Creek—from its headwaters to the west fork of the Calcasieu River in Beauregard and Calcasieu parishes (4) Bundicks Creek—from its headwaters to Bundick Lake and from Bundick Lake to Ouiska Chitto Creek in Vernon, Beauregard and Allen parishes (5) Hickory Branch—from its headwaters to the west fork of the Calcasieu River.

These acts only represent a few of the laws which were passed during the session affecting the public who utilize the natural resources of the state and the department. Several task forces, boards and advisory groups were also created to help increase public participation in the law and rule making advisory process. For a complete version of acts passed during the 2004 regular session of the Louisiana Legislature, visit their web site at: *www.legis.state.la.us*. The Department of Wildlife and Fisheries will also be updating our publications and issuing news releases to keep the citizens of our state informed of changes which occurred.

Employed by the Department of Wildlife and Fisheries since 1986, Major Jeff Mayne has worked as an enforcement agent for 14 years and has served as a legislative liaison for the past five years.

WISNER

WMA

Wildlife
MANAGEMENT AREA

Wisner Wildlife Management Area is located in south Lafourche Parish approximately 12 miles south of Leeville. Public launches available along Highway 1 facilitate boat access, and commercial ramps are located at Leeville and Grand Isle. Numerous waterways, bayous and canals offer good access to this 21,621-acre area owned by the Edward Wisner Donation Advisory Committee.

The terrain is mostly a low sub-delta saline marsh with scattered potholes, ponds and lakes. Major marsh vegetation is oyster grass, wire grass and salt grass. Widgeon grass is the major submergent, especially behind weirs which are most common in the Lake Laurier area. The few oak trees on the area are limited to the higher spoil banks along pipeline canals. Baccharis, iva, goldenrod and various grasses also grow on the spoil banks.

Burning patches of marsh grass in the winter is a method of habitat manipulation that has been used with success on Wisner. Not only are excess dead vegetation removed and valuable minerals recycled but new vegetation is immediately encouraged to grow by the practice of burning.

Game species hunted are mostly waterfowl, rabbit (on spoil banks), rails and snipe. Fur animals present are nutria, muskrat, mink, raccoon and otter.

Major fish species include speckled trout, redfish, flounder, black drum, sheepshead and croaker. Crabs and shrimp are also plentiful on the area. As always, be sure to check current regulations for dates and other information on hunting, trapping and fishing in this area.

The Brown Pelican is a regular visitor to Wisner. Many forms of recreation are available on the area including boating, bird watching, crabbing and shrimping. Additional information may be obtained from the Louisiana Department of Wildlife and Fisheries, P.O. Box 98000, Baton Rouge, LA 70898 or by phone at 225/765-2360.

North American
River Otter
(*Lutra canadensis*).

LDWF File Photo

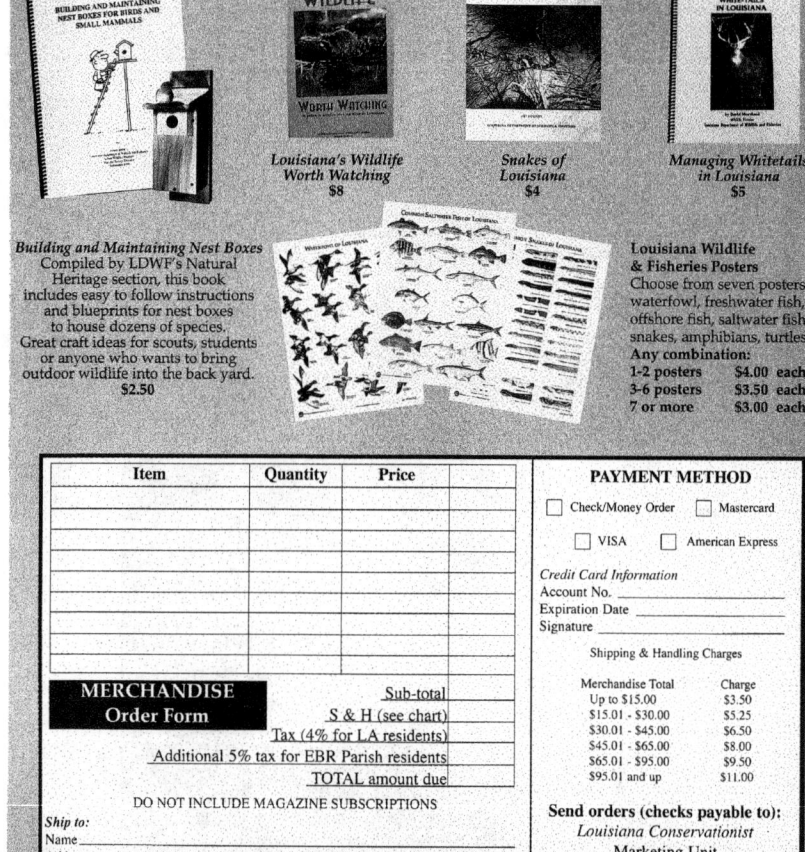

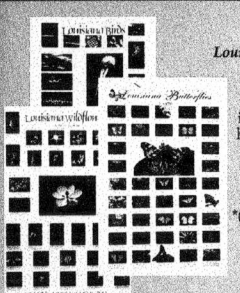
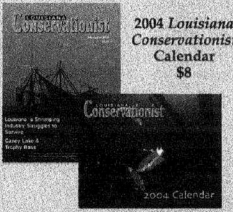

LAW lines

BY MAJ. KEITH LACAZE

Wildlife Management Area Regulations

The Louisiana Department of Wildlife and Fisheries offers public hunting, fishing and other outdoor recreational opportunities on 50 wildlife management areas (WMAs) located throughout the state. What are wildlife management areas? Management areas are lands owned and/or operated by LDWF. These lands are managed to provide wildlife habitat for the protection and propagation of a wide variety of species and to provide hunting and fishing opportunities for the public.

WMAs differ from state refuges by providing both public hunting and fishing, while the refuges offer fishing only. As one might expect, the hunting seasons on WMAs are abbreviated and differ from outside general season dates in order to protect wildlife from overharvest. Other special regulations are also in effect on the WMAs. The rules and regulations on the WMAs are approved and adopted by the Louisiana Wildlife and Fisheries Commission. These rules and regulations are in place for the protection of wildlife and the land, as well as for public safety and fair sharing of the area.

With hunting seasons approaching, this installment will examine some of the WMA rules and regulations and explain their purposes. We will also look at common violations of the rules and how to avoid those violations.

A hunting permit is required to hunt on all WMAs. The cost of this license is $15 and it is required for those aged 18 through 59, in addition to all other applicable hunting licenses. Remember, it is only required to hunt on a WMA. Those using WMAs for activities other than hunting or fishing, such as camping, shooting on rifle ranges, birdwatching and similar activities, must possess a valid Wild Louisiana Stamp, a valid fishing license or a valid hunting license. Persons under 16 and over 60 are exempt from this requirement.

The next permit required is the daily self clearing permit. Daily permits are required for managed hunts and are obtained at permit stations on or near the WMA entrance. The hunter's license is submitted to department personnel who provide the permit for the day. Upon checkout, the hunter returns the daily permit and picks up his license. Checkout is no later than two hours after sunset. Self clearing permits are obtained at unmanned information stations and are required for all activities.

The self clearing permit must be used at all times except during the managed hunts when daily permits are in effect. The self clearing permit consists of three parts: check in, check out and vehicle tag. Complete the check in portion and place it in the permit box before each day's activity on that day. Leave the vehicle portion visible on the dashboard of the vehicle driven into the WMA. Keep the check out portion on your person until leaving the WMA, when it is dropped in the permit box. Those hunting from camps have 72 hours from check in to drop the check out portion at the box. Those fishermen entering and leaving the WMA by boat are not required to obtain the self clearing permit.

Permitted hours of activity on WMAs are from two hours before legal shooting time until two hours after sunset. Entering the WMA during the night by boat to claim a duck hunting spot has been known to happen. This is illegal and creates hazardous boating conditions for other duck hunters who enter the area during legal hours before shooting time.

The daily deer limit on WMAs differs from the daily limit on private land. This situation has created some confusion and resulted in citations for over the limit of deer on some WMAs. On private land, the daily limit on deer is one antlered and one antlerless deer per day. On WMAs, the limit is one deer per day. More than one hunter has been cited for taking over the limit of deer on a WMA because he incorrectly thought the private land limit applied. Also, remember that during managed hunts, deer may not be skinned or have any external body parts removed before being checked out of the WMA.

Hunter requirements on the WMA differ from those on private lands too. All hunters except waterfowl and mourning dove hunters must wear both a hunter orange vest and cap during open gun season for deer. A minimum of an orange cap is required for hunters during special dog seasons for rabbit and squirrel. On legally posted private land, only an orange cap is required and may be removed when hunting from an elevated stand. Remember, hunter orange may not be removed even when hunting from an elevated stand on WMAs.

Other safety factors need to be considered when hunting on WMAs. The woods may be crowded at times and not everyone is as careful as they should be. When moving into a hunting area before daylight or leaving after dark, use a flashlight. It will not only light the way but will let other hunters know you are not a deer moving through. If an approaching hunter is unaware of your presence, get his or her attention by speaking while he or she is still some distance away. Avoid an unwelcome startled response, which may include having a gun pointed in your direction. Check the downrange area from your hunting location and make sure another hunter is not in the line of fire.

Firearms must be unloaded while being transported in boats and vehicles on WMAs. This is not merely a safety suggestion; it is a regulation and many people are cited each year for violating it. All guns should be unloaded as a safety precaution in boats and vehicles. But in the WMAs, the regulation is in place to further prohibit hunting from moving vehicles and boats.

The final word on WMA regulations involves littering. For some reason, many of our WMAs are favorite locations for illegal dumping. Tons of garbage, including old furniture, appliances and household trash, are deposited on our WMAs each year. The costs of cleaning up illegal dumpsites takes money away from wildlife management and habitat improvement projects on these WMAs. Law enforcement investigations of littering offenses take away from patrol hours better spent apprehending poachers.

Read the Louisiana Hunting Season and Wildlife Management Area Regulations booklet for a complete listing of all WMA regulations and season dates. Report violations of any WMA regulations to your nearest wildlife enforcement agent or call the 24-hour Louisiana Operation Game Thief Hotline at 800/442-2511. Cash rewards are paid for information leading to the issuance of citations or arrest of violators.

Broad-winged Hawk
Buteo platypterus

Within the hawk family Accipitridae, which includes kites, eagles and harriers, the Broad-winged Hawk is in a group known as buteos. Buteos are medium-to-large, thick-set hawks with broad, rounded wings and short-to-medium, fan-shaped tails. They hunt by soaring and circling high in the air or flying out after perching motionless on exposed perches.

Broad-winged Hawks often migrate in numbers along ridges and feed largely on rodents. Genus Buteo includes Red-tailed, Red-shouldered, Swainson's, Rough-legged and Harris' hawks.

As birds of prey, these hawks are equipped with powerful grasping

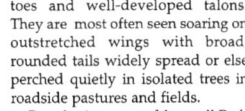

toes and well-developed talons. They are most often seen soaring on outstretched wings with broad, rounded tails widely spread or else perched quietly in isolated trees in roadside pastures and fields.

Broad-wings resemble small Red-tails, except that their tails are banded with brown and white. Most are distinctly smaller than Red-shouldered Hawks. Adult Broad-winged Hawks display underparts that are heavily mottled and barred, usually a dull brown in color.

Additionally, their rounded tails contain three or four wide, distinct black tail bands which are separated by narrower white bands. To identify these hawks, look for their short, broad wings, somewhat pointed at the tips, and a typical wingspan of 33 inches.

In Louisiana, Broad-winged Hawks nest in extensive, mature upland forests. In addition to those found in the heavily-forested portions of state, many Broad-winged Hawks migrate through Louisiana during the spring and fall. *Buteo platypterus* is most numerous in our state during September and October when these migratory flights are passing through.

A woodland species, Broad-winged Hawks mainly feed on rats, mice, reptiles, frogs and insects; they rarely catch small birds. Their nests, typically poorly-assembled constructions of sticks, leaves and bark, are usually found in the main crotches of deciduous trees or, if in pine trees, on horizontal branches next to the trunk. Usually only two eggs, similiar to those of Red-shouldered Hawks, are laid.

CONSERVATION
notes

BP PRESENTS LDWF WITH CHECK FOR ARTIFICIAL REEF

Representatives from BP America presented the Louisiana Department of Wildlife and Fisheries with a donation to the Louisiana Artificial Reef Program (LARP). The other portion of the donation now sits at the bottom of the Gulf of Mexico in the form of two sunken petroleum platforms.

The sunken platforms will now continue to be an important part of the fisheries habitat in the area. The area around this particular platform, known as Eugene Island 322, has particularly high levels of gag grouper and scamp, according to LARP Manager Rick Kasprzak.

The new artificial reef is located in the Eugene Island area, approximately 90 miles south of Marsh Island. The coordinates are 28 degrees, 17 minutes and 22 seconds North; 91 degrees, 21 minutes and 04 seconds West.

ENFORCEMENT AGENT SALPIETRA HONORED

Lieutenant Donald Salpietra of the Louisiana Department of Wildlife and Fisheries Enforcement Division was honored as Enforcement Officer of the Year at the 6th Annual Law Enforcement Day celebration held in Opelousas on May 15.

The St. Landry Parish Committee for Better Law Enforcement sponsors the annual event. Lieutenant Salpietra, who serves as the field supervisor for St. Landry, West Baton Rouge, Lafayette and Pointe Coupee parishes, was selected by his supervisors for outstanding contributions in his field.

CHANGES TO 2005 DUCK STAMP COMPETITION

Instead of featuring a specific duck or goose as has been done in each of the past 16 years of the program, the department is initiating a multiple year "Retrievers Save Game" series beginning with the 2005 competition. This year the black labrador retriever will be featured. The black lab must be prominent in the design and each entry must also include live waterfowl, selected by the artist. Artists may also choose to include harvested waterfowl in their art with duck decoys, hunting scenes and other backgrounds along with wetland habitats.

Entries for the competition will be accepted from October 18 until 4 p.m. on October 22. For more information on applying, judging and other contest guidelines, contact Robert Helm at 225/765-2358.

LDWF WINS GRANT FOR WETLAND CONSERVATION

The Louisiana Department of Wildlife and Fisheries received a national honor thanks to a grant from a groundbreaking partnership between Banrock Station Wines and The Conservation Fund.

LDWF was awarded a grant in the amount of $3,500 for its wetland conservation program dealing with Manchac Wildlife Management Area located in St. John Parish. LDWF, Southeastern Louisiana University and the Louisiana Department of Natural Resources have partnered with an ongoing wetland restoration and protection project that utilizes recycled Christmas trees.

TWO COMMISSIONERS APPOINTED TO LWFC

Governor Kathleen Blanco has announced the appointment of two new commissioners to the Louisiana Wildlife and Fisheries Commission. Robert Samanie, III, of Houma was appointed as the Shrimp/Coastal

Representative to the commission. He replaces Billy Broussard and his term will run through December 10, 2009. Earl P. King, Jr., of Amelia was appointed as a Coastal Representative and replaces Lee Felterman. King's term will run concurrent with the Governor.

NEW ASSISTANT SECRETARY AT WILDLIFE & FISHERIES

Governor Kathleen Babineaux Blanco has appointed W. Parke Moore, III, as the Assistant Secretary for the Office of Wildlife at the Department of Wildlife and Fisheries.

Moore brings nine years of state service to the agency, serving most recently as manager of Rosedown Plantation State Historic Site for the Office of State Parks. His 14 years in the private sector included management positions for environmental consulting firms and staff biologist project support at Howard, Needles, Tammen & Bergendoff (HNTB).

Moore, a graduate of Louisiana State University, earned a Bachelor of Science Degree in Forestry (1977) and a Master of Science Degree in Wildlife Management (1981).

MORELAND NAMED WILDLIFE DIVISION ADMINISTRATOR

Long-time Louisiana Deer Study Leader Dave Moreland has been named the new Wildlife Division Administrator for the Louisiana Department of Wildlife and Fisheries. Moreland is replacing Tommy Prickett, who retired from the position in May.

Moreland has been with the department since 1976, when he was hired as a biologist in District 7. He became the District 7 Game Division Supervisor in 1978 and served in that capacity until 1992, when he was named Deer Study Leader. Moreland has become well known and regarded in this position, both in Louisiana and across the southeastern portion of the country.

Dave Moreland graduated from Northeast Louisiana University with his bachelor's degree in biology and wildlife management and his master's degree in biology. He has authored dozens of publications regarding his work with the Louisiana deer herd and other topics and is a member of several wildlife organizations.

Louisiana Department of Wildlife and Fisheries Secretary Dwight Landreneau expressed his confidence in the Division Administrator saying, "Dave Moreland is very respected in his field and we are sure that he will bring professionalism and enthusiasm to this new position. We are very fortunate to have someone of his caliber heading our Wildlife Division, and the state's hunters will benefit from his expertise."

NEW BOAT LAUNCH OPENS AT POINTE-AUX-CHENES WMA

The Louisiana Department of Wildlife and Fisheries opened a new public boat launch area within the Pointe-Aux-Chenes Wildlife Management Area on Tuesday, Aug. 10.

The facility, over a third of a mile in length, will provide parking for 200 vehicles. Two dual-lane launches were constructed at each end of the parking area. The northernmost launch provides access to the St. Louis Canal with the south end ramp providing access into the marsh on the east side of La. 665. Project construction included a bridge across Bayou Pointe Au Chene.

The $900,000 project costs were paid for with federal Coastal Impact Assistance Program funds and a Rockefeller Refuge Fund allocation. Lowland Construction Company of Thibodaux was the contractor.

To reach the launch area from Houma, take La. 24 south to La. 55, turning left at La. 665. Continue to the bridge across Bayou Pointe Au Chene approximately one-half mile south of the Pointe-Aux Chenes WMA headquarters on La. 665.

CAPT. JUBAL MARCEAUX TO COMMAND ENFORCEMENT REGION V

LDWF Secretary Dwight Landreneau and Enforcement Division Administrator Colonel Winton Vidrine have announced the promotion of Lt. Jubal Marceaux to the rank of captain. Marceaux will supervise LDWF Enforcement Division's Region V, covering the parishes of Allen, Beauregard, Evangeline, Calcasieu, Cameron, Acadia, Vermilion and Jefferson Davis.

Marceaux is a 13-year veteran of the Enforcement Division and had previously served as the supervisor of the Refuge Patrol Section. He studied criminal justice at the University of Southwestern Louisiana before joining the Enforcement Division in 1991. He replaces Capt. Malcolm Hebert as the region supervisor. Hebert retired in March of this year.

SGT. LAVIOLETTE NAMED WILDLIFE ENFORCEMENT AGENT OF THE YEAR

LDWF Enforcement Sergeant Todd Laviolette was named the LDWF Enforcement Agent of the Year at the 2004 Louisiana Wildlife Agents Association Conference on July 31 in Houma.

Col. Winton Vidrine, Law Enforcement Division Administrator, cited Laviolette's 14 years of hard work and dedication as an agent and his participation in teaching boating safety and hunter education classes while presenting the award.

Sgt. Laviolette is the Region VIII evidence custodian and a member of the Wildlife Enforcement Dive Team.

Todd and his wife Angelle reside in Chalmette with their two children, Justin and Casey. He will attend the Southeastern Association of Fish and Wildlife Agencies Conference this fall in South Carolina, representing Louisiana.

STATEMENT OF OWNERSHIP, MANAGEMENT AND CIRCULATION
(Required by 39 U.S.C. 3685)
1. Publication title: Louisiana Conservationist
2. Publication No.: 246778
3. Filing date: 10/1/04
4. Issue frequency: bi-monthly
5. No. of issues published annually: 6
6. Annual subscription rate: $12
7. Complete mailing address of known office of publication: 2000 Quail Dr., Baton Rouge, LA 70808.
8. Complete mailing address of headquarters of general business officer of publisher: 2000 Quail Dr., Baton Rouge, LA 70808.
9. Full names and complete mailing addresses of publisher, editor and managing editor: Publisher, Louisiana Department of Wildlife and Fisheries, 2000 Quail Dr., Baton Rouge, LA 70808; Editor, Thomas Gresham, 2000 Quail Dr., Baton Rouge, LA 70808; Managing Editor, Jill Wilson, 2000 Quail Dr., Baton Rouge, LA 70808.
10. Owner: Louisiana Department of Wildlife and Fisheries (nonprofit) 2000 Quail Dr., Baton Rouge, LA 70808; mailing address, P.O. Box 98000, Baton Rouge, LA 70898; no stockholders.
11. Known bondholders, mortgagees and other security holders owning or holding 1 percent or more of total amount of bonds, mortgages or other securities: none.
12. For completion by nonprofit organizations authorized to mail at special rates. The purpose, function and nonprofit status of this organization and the exempt status for federal income tax purposes: has not changed during the preceding 12 months.
13. Publication name: Louisiana Conservationist
14. Issue date for circulation data below: 9/1/04
15. Extent and nature of circulation:
    Average number copies each issue during preceding 12 months:
    A. Total no. copies (net press run): 22,540
    B. Paid and/or requested circulation:
        1. Sales through dealers and carrier, street vendors and counter sales (not mailed): none
        2. Paid or requested mail subscriptions (include advertisers proof copies/exchange copies): 22,540
    C. Total paid and/or requested circulation (sum of 15b-1 and 15b-2): 22,540
    D. Free distribution by mail (samples, complimentary and other free): none
    E. Free distribution outside the mail (carriers or other means): none
    F. Total free distribution (sum of 15d and 15e): none
    G. Total distribution (sum of 15c and 15f): 22,540
    H. Copies not distributed:
        1. Office use, leftovers, spoiled: none
        2. Return from news agents: none
    I. Total (sum of 15g, 15h-1 and 15h-2): 22,540
        Percent paid and/or requested circulation: 100
    Actual no. copies of single issue published nearest to filing date:
    A. Total no. copies (net press run): 22,540
    B. Paid and/or requested circulation:
        1. Sales through dealers and carrier, street vendors and counter sales (not mailed): none
        2. Paid or requested mail subscriptions (include advertisers proof copies/ exchange copies): 22,540
    C. Total paid and/or requested circulation (sum of 15b-1 and 15b-2): 22,540
    D. Free distribution by mail (samples, complimentary and other free): none
    E. Free distribution outside the mail (carriers or other means): none
    F. Total free distribution (sum of 15d and 15e): none
    G. Total distribution (sum of 15c and 15f): 23,980
    H. Copies not distributed:
        1. Office use, leftovers, spoiled: none, none
        2. Return from news agents: none
    I. Total (sum of 15g, 15h-1 and 15h-2): 22,540
        Percent paid and/or requested circulation: 100
16. This statement of ownership will be printed in the Sept./Oct. 2004 issue of this publication.
17. Signature and title of editor: Thomas Gresham, Editor
I certify that all information furnished on this form is true and complete. I understand that anyone who furnishes false or misleading information on this form or who omits material or information requested on the form may be subject to criminal sanctions (including fines and imprisonment) and/or civil sanctions (including multiple damages and civil penalties).

Along the Way...

Spots in My Eyes

By Pete Cooper Jr.

Throughout my life I've had this "thing" about fly fishing for bass in flowing water, and at times it compels me to do just that, pre-empting even a hot saltwater opportunity. I assume its foundation is a gorgeous creek that ran through my maternal grandparents' ranch in the Texas Hill Country where at around age 10 I caught my first bass on a fly—the first of many from its sparkling waters.

Back then I also had the opportunity to fly fish the nearby Medina River. There I caught some strange-looking bass which I assumed were supercharged largemouths but which many decades later I discovered were Guadeloupe bass—a distinct species. I was impressed!

My grandfather sold that ranch just as I turned 14, and for two years I caught very few bass in flowing water. One of note came from the old Caddo Lake dam's spillway, and it looked—and acted—a lot like the bass I had caught in Hill Country rivers. That day I was with my baseball coach, and he identified the fish as a spotted bass. Again I was impressed!

While I did catch a few more of them on subsequent trips to the dam, spots began to play a much larger role in my life after I graduated from high school. Then I would often car-top my new duckboat to Bayou Dorcheat and catch them near Dixie Inn—wonderfully pretty water back then—on both conventional crankbaits and fly-rod poppers.

Spots also came in surprise packages. One misty, early-April morning while I was on Easter break from LSU, I found them on Lake Bistineau's Pin Oak Flats, apparently spawning. Those were the largest I had ever encountered, and they crawled all over my surface lure. There was also the monster that a frat brother caught in a bar-pit alongside Two O'Clock Bayou. And I'll never forget the surprise I got from the single, quite respectable spot I caught on a deeply-worked crankbait one slick, hot August evening while fishing the oxbow lake just across the levee from LSU-S—the only one I ever

caught in that once-upon-a-time honey-hole.

Spots also schooled with barfish in Caddo and Bistineau, and during an early-autumn drawdown of Bistineau, Barbara and I—married barely a month—found a gang of them in a shallow boat-road off Bossier Slough. Those, like the spawners, went wild over surface lures. I'll never forget that evening: calm, clear black water reflecting the reddening cypresses, the music of arriving geese, the occasional plaintive cries of nutrias and newlyweds in the duckboat, catching spotted bass on topwaters. Somewhere it may get better than that—somewhere.

That could only be in flowing water, and in the spring of 1966 I met the Comite River. It was discovered, I must confess, on an afternoon softball game along its sandy shoreline. Not long thereafter I made a scouting run with a fly rod and discovered that it indeed held spots.

The Comite in the reach above and below the Greenwell Springs Road was a deceiving little creek. Much of it was comprised of shallow riffles across a sand and pea-gravel substrate. Mid-stream pockets deep enough to hold bass were bathed in sunlight most of the day, and any bass that might have been in them seldom cooperated. But find a subtle little washout along a shoreline which was shaded by overhanging limbs, or fish under a heavy overcast or after sunset, and it was a real jewel.

And it glistened even brighter that autumn with color in the shoreline hardwoods and a bit of a chill in the water. I absolutely loved it!

The following spring I met Barbara, and we soon made our first trip to the Comite together. There were some people swimming near the bridge when we arrived, even though a light rain was falling. We worked our way upstream for a short distance, and had two nice spots oblige, before the rain became a deluge, the river began to rise and we decided to get the heck out of Dodge. Almost back to LSU, we

heard the guy on the radio say two people had just drowned in the Comite River near the Greenwell Springs Road. Even pretty little creeks can get really nasty sometimes.

She and I were married that September, and for many years there-after I fly fished for bass in flowing water only during brief vacations to visit her folks in Missouri. It's a different world up there—clear, cool water, big hills and smallmouths. I became enamored with the brown bass and the environment surrounding them, and for two decades I ignored Louisiana's creeks and their spots, limiting my local fly-fishing efforts almost entirely toward saltwater targets.

Eventually some fly-guys in New Orleans informed me of a pretty little creek north of Bogalusa that I might like to try. The initial scouting run resulted in two of the largest spots I had ever taken, and the fact that I caught them on a crankbait did not prevent me from almost exclusively fly fishing it thereafter—Pushepatapa Creek. It was a beautiful place back then—still is—and it holds perhaps the largest spots of any of Louisiana's scenic streams. Indeed, that's where my state record fly-caught spot came from, and that's where I was confronted with an environmental issue that led to my meeting Keith Cascio, the coordinator of the System and now a great friend and fly-fishing buddy.

Since then we have "surveyed and random sampled" several of the state's scenic streams, most of which have shown evidence of a good population of spotted bass. One—Kisatchie Bayou—has grown in endearment to a level almost equaling that of the "Pushe"—it has real, honest-to-God rocks in it as well as a lot of nice spots. And it, too, is a pretty "scenic stream."

I'd have to say most of those that hold spots in Louisiana are pretty—at least most of those that Keith and I have "surveyed and random sampled." (That's scientific terminology for "fly fished in a creek.") And that's part of the appeal of it all. Yeah, I'll take a spot anywhere and in any way I can catch it, I will appreciate and admire it for what it is and then I will probably release it. But when I catch one from flowing water on a fly-rod popper, I always feel I've been treated to something special.

And I hope that feeling never changes.

1/2 vidalia onion, thinly sliced
1 clove garlic, minced
1/4 c. olive oil
1 Tbsp. chopped parsley
1/2 medium bell pepper, sliced
3 spears asparagus

Prepare the fettuccini and set it aside. Heat half the oil. Coat tuna with pecans and sear. Saute shrimp and remaining ingredients. Salt and pepper to taste.

Assembly: Place fettuccini in the center of the plate atop the asparagus bottoms. Place tuna on top. Top tuna with shrimp; spoon tomatoes and sauce over it.

Mixed Baby Green Salad With Port Wine Vinaigrette

1 c. mixed green salad, cleaned
1/4 cucumber, sliced
4 grape tomatoes, sliced in half
1 tsp. grated parmesan cheese
1/2 c. olive oil

1/4 c. port wine
1/4 clove garlic, minced
salt & pepper to taste

Assemble the salad. Combine wine and garlic. Blend oil in gradually. Salt and pepper to taste. Serve over salad.

Tasty Taylor Toast

4 thick slices of frenchbread
3 Tbsp. butter, softened
1/4 clove garlic, minced
4 slices Mozzarella cheese
4 slices beef steak tomatoes

Heat oven to 400 degrees. Combine butter and garlic, then spread over sliced frenchbread. Place one slice of cheese on each piece of bread and top with tomato. Place in the oven until golden brown.

Chef Celeste Gill is the owner of TaylorMade Gourmet Foods in Baton Rouge.

CPSIA information can be obtained
at www.ICGtesting.com
Printed in the USA
BVHW041755301118
534322BV00030B/225/P